Rhode Island

BY HOLLY SAARI

Published by The Child's World®
1980 Lookout Drive • Mankato, MN 56003-1705
800-599-READ • www.childsworld.com

ACKNOWLEDGMENTS
The Child's World®: Mary Berendes, Publishing Director
The Design Lab: Design and production
Red Line Editorial: Editorial direction

PHOTO CREDITS: Stuart Monk/Bigstock, cover, 1, 3; Matt Kania/Map Hero,
Inc., 4, 5; Myles Dumas/iStockphoto, 7; John Archer/iStockphoto, 9; 123RF,
10; Michael Hare/Shutterstock Images, 11; Steven Senne/AP Images, 13;
North Wind Picture Archives/Photolibrary, 15; Sheldon Kralstein/iStockphoto,
17; Paul Drinkwater/AP Images, 19; Larry Ebbs/iStockphoto, 21; One Mile
Up, 22; Quarter-dollar coin image from the United States Mint, 22

LIBRARY OF CONGRESS CATALOGING-IN-PUBLICATION DATA
Saari, Holly.
  Rhode Island / by Holly Saari.
       p. cm.
  Includes bibliographical references and index.
  ISBN 978-1-60253-484-1 (library bound : alk. paper)
  1. Rhode Island—Juvenile literature. I. Title.

F79.3.S23 2010
974.5—dc22

                    2010019324

Printed in the United States of America in Mankato, Minnesota.
July 2010
F11538

On the cover:
Castle Hill
Lighthouse
is in Newport,
Rhode Island.

CONTENTS

Geography

Let's explore Rhode Island! Rhode Island is in the northeastern United States. This area is called New England. Rhode Island has the smallest land area of any state.

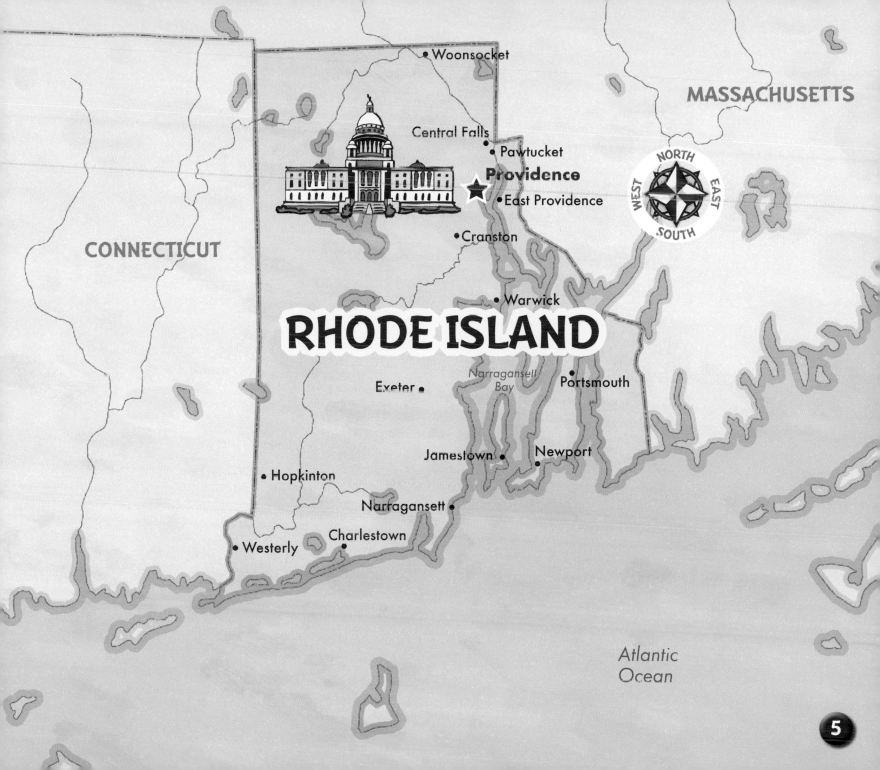

MASSACHUSETTS

CONNECTICUT

Woonsocket

Central Falls

Pawtucket

Providence

East Providence

Cranston

NORTH

WEST EAST

SOUTH

Warwick

RHODE ISLAND

Narragansett Bay

Exeter

Portsmouth

Jamestown

Newport

Hopkinton

Narragansett

Charlestown

Westerly

Atlantic Ocean

Cities

Providence is the capital of Rhode Island. It is the largest city in the state. It is a **port**. Warwick is another well-known city.

Rhode Island only has eight cities. It has 31 towns. Towns are smaller than cities.

Providence is home to about 175,000 people. ▶

Land

Rhode Island's land is flat in the south near the ocean. This part of the state has beaches, too. The west is hilly. Rhode Island also has lakes and ponds.

Some parts of Rhode Island's coastline are rocky. ▶

Plants and Animals

Rhode Island has many forests. The state tree is the red maple. The state flower is the violet. Many animals live in Rhode Island's woods. These include foxes, deer, and rabbits. Pheasants live in the state, too. The state bird is the Rhode Island Red. It is a kind of chicken.

Rhode Island was the last state to adopt a state flower. ▶

People and Work

About 1 million people live in Rhode Island. Rhode Island is known for producing jewelry and silverware. **Tourism** is also important to the state. Medicines and **chemicals** are made in Rhode Island. The state has many bankers and people who work in **finance**. Others work in fishing, farming, and **manufacturing**.

Some people in Rhode Island work in health-care jobs, such as nursing. ▶

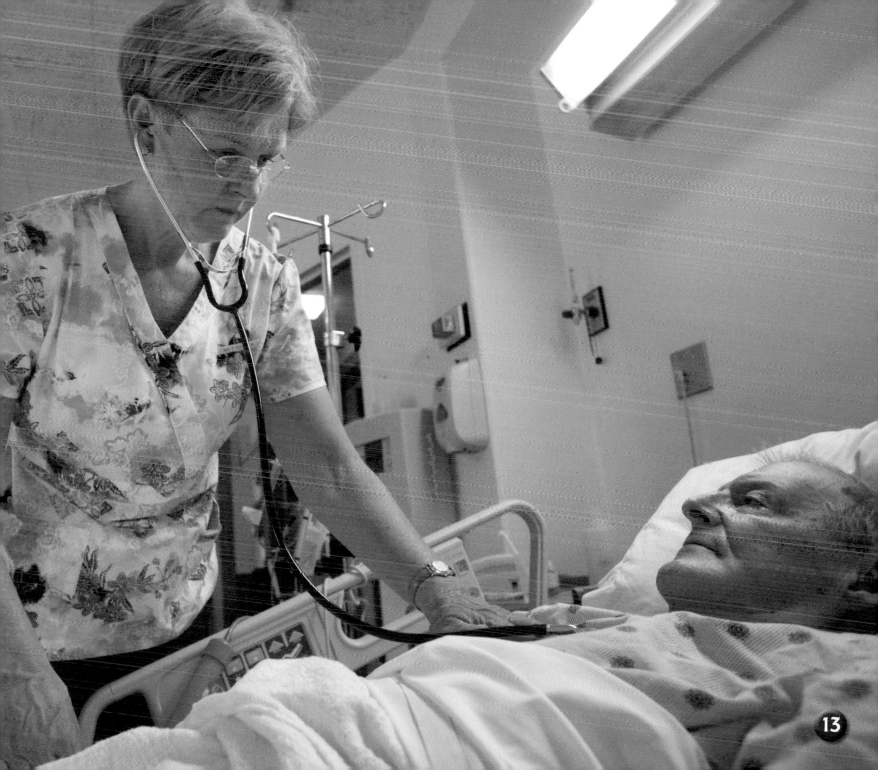

History

Native Americans have lived in the Rhode Island area for thousands of years. Settlers from Europe came to the area in the 1630s. They wanted to practice their **religions** in peace. Rhode Island became the thirteenth state on May 29, 1790.

Roger Williams founded the **colony** of Rhode Island. ▶

15

Ways of Life

There are many things to do around the water in Rhode Island. People enjoy boating, fishing, and swimming. The state is a **popular** place for boat racing.

Music is important in Rhode Island, too. The Newport Jazz Festival takes place here every summer.

Sailing is popular in Rhode Island. ▶

Famous People

Writer Jhumpa Lahiri grew up in Rhode Island, and writer Cormac McCarthy was born in the state. They both have won important prizes for their work. H. P. Lovecraft is a horror writer from the state. Actress Debra Messing grew up in Rhode Island, and television news host Meredith Vieira was born in the state.

Meredith Vieira was born in Providence. ▶

Famous Places

Rhode Island is known for the area named Narragansett **Bay**. It is about 28 miles (45 km) long. There are many islands in this area. The bay makes Rhode Island an unusual shape. There are many large, old houses in Newport, a city on the bay. Visitors can tour some of these homes.

The Breakers is a famous Newport house that was home to the Vanderbilt family. ▶

State Symbols

Seal

Rhode Island's seal has an **anchor**. This shows the state's focus on the ocean. Go to **childsworld.com/links** for a link to Rhode Island's state Web site, where you can get a firsthand look at the state seal.

Flag

Rhode Island's flag has the word *hope*. That is the state's **motto**.

Quarter

Rhode Island's state quarter has a sailboat on it. The quarter came out in 2001.

Glossary

anchor (ANG-kur): An anchor is a heavy object that is dropped in the water to keep a boat in place. An anchor is on the Rhode Island state seal.

bay (BAY): A bay is a small body of water partially surrounded by land and connected to a larger body of water. Rhode Island has a bay named Narragansett Bay.

chemicals (KEM-uh-kulz): Chemicals are substances used in chemistry. Some chemicals are produced in Rhode Island.

colony (KOL-uh-nee): A colony is an area of land that is newly settled and is controlled by a government of another land. Roger Williams founded the Rhode Island colony.

festival (FESS-tih-vul): A festival is a celebration for an event or holiday. The Newport Jazz Festival in Rhode Island celebrates music.

finance (FYE-nanss): Finance is a group of businesses that take care of money. Some people in Rhode Island work in finance.

lighthouse (LYT-howss): A lighthouse is a tall building near an ocean or large lake that uses lights to warn ships of danger. Castle Hill Lighthouse is in Rhode Island.

manufacturing (man-yuh-FAK-chur-ing): Manufacturing is the task of making items with machines. Some people in Rhode Island work in manufacturing.

motto (MOT-oh): A motto is a sentence that states what people stand for or believe. Rhode Island's motto appears on the state flag.

popular (POP-yuh-lur): To be popular is to be enjoyed by many people. Sailing and other water activities are popular in Rhode Island.

port (PORT): A port is a city on a body of water to which ships travel. Providence is a port.

religions (reh-LIJ-unz): Religions are systems of beliefs about God or gods. People came to Rhode Island to have freedom to practice their religions.

seal (SEEL): A seal is a symbol a state uses for government business. Rhode Island's seal has an anchor on it.

symbols (SIM-bulz): Symbols are pictures or things that stand for something else. The seal and flag are Rhode Island's symbols.

tourism (TOOR-ih-zum): Tourism is visiting another place (such as a state or country) for fun or the jobs that help these visitors. Tourism is important in Rhode Island.

Further Information

Books

Keller, Laurie. *The Scrambled States of America*. New York: Henry Holt, 2002.

Martonyi, E. Andrew. *The Little Man In the Map: With Clues To Remember All 50 States*. Woodland Hills, CA: Schoolside Press, 2007.

Thornton, Brian. *The Everything Kids' States Book: Wind Your Way Across Our Great Nation*. Avon, MA: Adams Media, 2007.

Web Sites

Visit our Web site for links about Rhode Island: *childsworld.com/links*

Note to Parents, Teachers, and Librarians: We routinely verify our Web links to make sure they are safe and active sites. So encourage your readers to check them out!

Index